And You Call Yourself a Christian?

The Danger of Self-Deception and Disobedience

Danielle Milano

WestBow Press
PRESS
A DIVISION OF THOMAS NELSON

WestBow Press books may be ordered through booksellers or by contacting:

WestBow Press
A Division of Thomas Nelson
1663 Liberty Drive
Bloomington, IN 47403
www.westbowpress.com
1-(866) 928-1240

ISBN: 978-1-4497-6209-4 (sc)

Library of Congress Control Number: 2012914101

Printed in the United States of America

WestBow Press rev. date: 09/20/2012

Contents

Acknowledgements

First and Foremost, to my Heavenly Father, to the Son, and the Holy Spirit, for loving me when I was at my most unlovable, for saving me, for choosing me, and for teaching me (even when I would rather be asleep!)....Thank You.

To my mother, LaJetta McDaniel, who set a firm foundation under me and prayed for me when I was "too smart" to pray......You are priceless! I thank you.

To my father, Rev. Ron McDaniel....you set a good example. As often as I think of how God changed you and see how He uses you now....it is an inspiration. I thank you.

To my husband, Ramon Milano.....for believing in me and supporting me.....I thank you. We've come a long way together and I am glad that you are mine and I am yours.

To my sister Dia Johnson.....you don't even know how you've helped me.....you've always been there and I thank you for it.

Last but not least, to my current and previous pastors: First to Rev. John J. Harris III, a wonderful teacher, I learned so much under you as I was growing up. Your labors have not been in vain. Second to Rev. Dion Greer, I still consider you and the Allen Chapel AME Church my "Connecticut family." We really had no one when we first moved there, so I thank you and the Allen Chapel church family for taking us in and loving us. I love you all and I am so grateful to God for you. Last, to Pastors Greg and Celeste Texada, under your ministry I feel I have grown in leaps and bounds. Sometimes I look back and I am amazed at who I used to be and who I am now. I give God the glory, but I thank you for your part. This book would not have been possible without you.

I am sure there are more I should be thanking, but my mind won't cooperate. For everyone who loved me, spoke good things over my life, supported and prayed for me.....I thank you.

Introduction

The Lord woke me up very early one morning during a time of prayer and fasting in my church. He gave me this book, with the purpose of waking up His people. When Jesus returns, he is looking for a church without spot or blemish. Obviously that does not mean perfection, as the body is filled with imperfect people. However, he is looking for people whose hearts are perfect toward him. This is where there is a problem. There are many people in the Church who think that they are okay with the Lord and they are not. Most are deceived, and some are hypocrites, walking in disobedience to God's word. Hopefully this book will reach both. Allow me to state my case. In a dying and hurting world, it is those of us in the Church who are meant to show God's love and minister to those who are lost. The problem is most of us are not fully submitted to God. We don't practice what we preach. Even those who are not saved call Christians hypocrites. It is one of the primary reasons that we have difficulty bringing the lost to Christ. Do you honestly think the enemy cares about whether or not you go to church when you still live in a way that is contrary to God's word? Not at all! He knows that church membership does not save us from our sins. Look at the well known scripture in James 1:22 (NIV): *"Do not merely listen to the word, and so deceive yourselves. Do what it says."* We are not okay by just being hearers. We have to be doers also. Take a look at Matthew 7:21 (NIV): *"Not everyone who says to me, 'Lord, Lord,' will enter the kingdom of heaven, <u>but only he who does the will of my Father who is in heaven"</u>* (underline added by author). Let me tell you my own story. I was a hypocrite. I grew up in the church. I knew God's word. When I graduated high school and went to college, I began to go my own way. I went to church to ease my conscious maybe once every three months on average. I didn't get drunk, do drugs or anything like that, but I was engaged in sexual sin and walked in pride. Five years after I graduated from high school, I was unmarried, living with my boyfriend, and we already had a child. I told the Lord that I knew what I was doing. I made all of my own decisions. One day I was on my way to work. There was a curve that I had driven hundreds of times before (and hundreds of times since) with no problems. However, on this day, I took the curve wrong. I took it too wide. I overcorrected, and the car slid on some gravel that was on the shoulder. I yanked the steering wheel back to the left, which resulted in my totally losing control of the car. I kept trying to remember all I had learned about driving like not to slam on my brakes, but I could not regain control. I recall just letting go of the steering wheel and covering my head. I felt a jolt and the car shook. When I opened my eyes, the car was upside down in a ditch. I could not open the car on the driver side because the ditch was very narrow. I tried the passenger side and it gave a little, but I was not strong enough on my own to push it past the dirt. I even tried kicking the glass out, but I couldn't do it. I was trapped and helpless, which is not a feeling I was accustomed to. I sat back and just looked around. I realized that the car was still running and I saw fluid coming out of the car. I began to think about all the movies I had seen about how people see fluid dripping just before the explosion (perhaps I've watched too many movies). I thought about my family, and my baby. I also thought about God. I realized that if I died, I would not be going to heaven, because my life was not in line with His word. The horror of dying in a burning car and then going to hell for all eternity overwhelmed me. It was then that I began screaming. I was still screaming when a guy came and opened the passenger door. Of course, the car never exploded. I was probably never in any danger, but God had to bring me to a place where I would see my true spiritual condition. I had to stop lying to myself about where I really stood with Him. My car was completely totaled, but I survived with just a scratch on my knee. People have died in lesser wrecks, so I know God was at work in that situation, and I thank Him for His mercy every day. I would be lying if I said that I cleaned up my life instantly, but that is where it began. I stopped justifying my sin (for example I would say things like in my mind my boyfriend was already my husband) and making excuses. It took awhile (I should also thank God for His patience) before we finally got things right. In truth, we had two children before we were married a day. That was not my only sin, just one of many. I believe he saw that I would make the choice to live for Him, so He was patient with me. However, we can't presume on God's patience forever. We can't just assume that a time will come and we will stop living our own lifestyles and follow Him. In truth, the longer we wait, the harder our hearts become. We have to stop playing with our eternal destiny. It's time to live for Him.

Chapter One: In Spirit and In Truth

John 4:21-24

True Worship

God seeks true worshippers. How can anyone who claims to be a true worshipper come before God when they still actively participate in sinful activity? Anyone who thinks God just looks the other way is gravely mistaken. When people say that "God is not a respecter of persons," they usually mean that God doesn't love anyone more or less than another. I think it also means that God doesn't make allowances for anyone. The penalty for my sin is the same as the penalty for yours. There are no favorites (Col 3:25). We don't get a "get out of Hell free" card. Jesus already paid that price, and he won't come back to die for those who choose to continue to live in sin. Why call him Lord when we do not do as He says? (taken from Luke 6:46 NIV). On the flip side, why call him Lord when we do things He said not to do? Jesus says in John 14:15 NIV, "If you love me, you will obey what I command." I wonder if we understand how serious this is. Think of Jesus' atoning death on the cross. Perhaps some of us are too cavalier about what He accomplished on the cross. This gift is sometimes accepted with no real thought to what it means and the price He paid. We see signs that give tribute to our veterans such as "freedom isn't free" and other similar slogans. This is true. We are redeemed. We have been freed from bondage to sin. However, that freedom was never free. Jesus paid a debt no one else could pay. It cost him his life, His blood. We are allowed to have fellowship with the Creator because of Jesus. THIS IS NOT A COMMON THING! So then the question becomes, why accept this gift, be cleansed of all our sins, and then go back to the same behavior? If a person is in prison and someone comes along with the keys and offers to open the door with no strings attached, would that person leave or stay? My guess is that person would leave (and not look back). Would the same person voluntarily go right back to prison? One would say no, right? That's what the vast majority do every day! We have been set free from sin. With God's help, we can overcome the desires of the flesh. We do this by learning God's word and living by it. When Jesus was tempted, He gave the perfect example. His response always began with "It is written....." That's how he fought off the temptation to sin. As for us, some of us are saved and then go back to the same behavior as if nothing ever happened. See what is said about this in Hebrews 10: 26-27 NIV: *"If we deliberately keep on sinning after we have received the knowledge of the truth, no sacrifice for sins is left, but only a fearful expectation of judgment and of raging fire that will consume the enemies of God."* Skip down to Hebrews 10:29-31 NIV: *"How much more severely do you think a man deserves to be punished who has trampled the Son of God under foot, who has treated as an unholy thing the blood of the covenant that sanctified him, and who has insulted the Spirit of grace? For we know him who said "It is mine to avenge; I will repay," and again "The*

Lord will judge his people." It is a dreadful thing to fall into the hands of the living God" (underline added by author). Refer to 2nd Peter 2:20-22, which speaks on the same thing. We call ourselves Christians, but our continued involvement in sinful activity indicates something entirely different. Obedience is the highest form of worship. Only those who obey God's word (written and spoken) and pattern their lives after it are true worshippers.

Spiritual Worship

"God is spirit and those that worship Him must do so in spirit and in truth," (paraphrased from John 4:24 NIV). Those are Jesus' words. To find an answer as to how to worship spiritually, go to Romans 12:1 NIV *"Therefore I urge you brothers, in view of God's mercy, to offer your bodies as living sacrifices, holy and pleasing to God-this is your spiritual act of worship."* What does it mean to present our bodies as living sacrifices? It means to give over our lives, our own desires, dreams, and plans, etc in essence our will. Instead of doing what we desire, we do what He desires. We seek to do His will. We "crucify our flesh," meaning we force our bodies to do God's will, and not our own. We are God's children, and he calls us to live holy lives, just as He is holy. We are meant to be sanctified, set apart. God chose Israel with the purpose of making her an example for all nations. The idea was to bless Israel so much that other nations would see, glorify God in heaven, and abandon their false gods. This is what God intended when he told Abraham that through his offspring all nations would be blessed. However, this was actually fulfilled in Jesus, as Israel was not able to keep the covenant they made with God. As His children, shouldn't we look like our father? In the natural, we look at our own children and talk about who they look or act like. It should be no different spiritually. One should be able to tell who your father is by your behavior and your lifestyle. Some of us claim that our father is God, but actually belong to the devil. This is nothing new, as Jesus told the religious leaders of his time that they were of their father the devil. How is it that there are people in the church who are of the devil? The simple answer is they don't heed James 1:22 NIV (see above). Some go to church and the word of God goes in one ear and out the other. There is no attempt to be a doer of the word. That's where self-deception and/or disobedience set in. Too many think that as long as they are in church hearing the word (but not doing or living by that word), they are okay with God. I once saw a church sign that says "God wants full custody, not weekend visits." We should follow Jesus' example. He only did his father's will and only said what he heard his father say. His word says that we are to be set apart. We are meant to be an example for all in the world to see. It is time to "throw off everything that hinders and the sin that so easily entangles," (taken from Hebrews 12:1 NIV). It is time to worship Him with our very lives, in spirit and in truth.

Chapter Two: Spotlight--
Acts of the Sinful Nature

Galatians 5:19-21

There is a need to shine a spotlight on sin as it is identified by the word of God. Hopefully in identifying sin, perhaps eyes will open and conviction and true repentance will be the result. We will primarily use the scripture referenced above, though there are more scriptures on sin and this is not an all inclusive list of the sins one can commit.

1) Sexual Immorality, Impurity and Debauchery-You're involved in this? Really? And you call yourself a Christian?

Apparently this is a huge one, because there are several scriptures that identify sin, and in most of them sexual immorality is named first, and it is listed somewhere in ALL of them. See the following in addition to the above referenced scripture: 1st Corinthians 6:9; Ephesians 5:3; Colossians 3:5; Revelations 21:8; and Revelation 22:15.

What is sexual immorality? Put plainly, it is any sort of sexual activity outside the area for which it was intended by God. Sex is intended only for marriage and that between a man and a woman. Anything outside of this is perversion. What is it about sex that has us so deceived? Why can't we control ourselves in this area? I was deceived also in this area if you will recall my story. Remember how I said that my life didn't change immediately (as it should have)? Both of my children were born before I was married a day. I was convinced that I was saved in spite of the sin(s) I was committing. I did not turn away even after the Lord began to deal with me about it. Perhaps it was lack of fear and too much reliance upon His grace and mercy that kept me from immediately shaping up. I am grateful for His deliverance, because I could be dead right now. I could be awaiting the second death simply because I was not obedient to God's word in at least that one area of my life. Most of us know that even one sin can separate us from God. Thank God for Jesus! I was going to church, attending bible study, singing in the choir, and even teaching children. None of that, however, would have erased the sin in my life. God, in His infinite mercy and patience, allowed me the time to get it right. He is still showing all of us His patience and mercy, which is supported by the fact that we are still here.

There are several types of sexual sin. They are as follows: adultery, which is a married person who has sex with someone other than his or her spouse (author's definition); prostitution, which is the act of soliciting and accepting payment for sex acts or the act of selling oneself for an unworthy purpose*; homosexuality, which is sex with someone of the same gender (author's definition); and bestiality, which is sex with an animal (author's definition and gross!). There are other activities in which sexual immorality is included: an orgy, which is a revel involving unrestrained indulgence, especially in sexual activity, or uncontrolled indulgence in an activity.* We can wrap all of these sins into one word: fornication.

Why is this a sin? For a Christian, the answer is obvious: because God says it is. Seriously, it is a sign of unfaithfulness, a lack of self-control, and it is an act of defilement. See Leviticus 18. When He commanded the Israelites not to do these things, He said that these acts were detestable. The land He promised them was inhabited by people engaged in these activities. He drove them out because of this and commanded holiness for the Israelites. He commands our holiness too, because He is holy and we are supposed to be like him. Think of all the possible effects: unwanted pregnancies (and the drama that results from it), diseases, divorces, etc all because we allow our flesh to control us instead of the other way around. It was never God's will for any of these things to happen to us.

Impurity and debauchery were included in this category because sexual sin is also involved in them. Impurity is defined as not clean, contaminated, immoral and obscene.* Debauchery means to corrupt morally or to reduce the quality of.* This is how God sees those who actively engage in sexual sin. Our bodies are the temple of the Holy Spirit. We are not meant to defile our bodies in any way. Don't deceive yourselves. Don't allow yourself to be deceived. If you are involved in sexual immorality of any sort, you will not inherit the kingdom of God, in spite of any good works or what you do in the church. See Hebrews 13:4NIV- *Marriage should be honored by all, and the marriage bed kept pure, for God will judge the adulterer and all the sexually immoral* (underline added by author).

2) Idolatry, Selfish Ambition, and Pride-
You're into this? Really? And you call yourself a Christian?

"You shall have no other gods before me." Exodus 20:3NIV. I put these particular sins together because both of them at their core mean putting something above God, be it another "god" or ourselves.

Idolatry-We know that idolatry is idol worship, but I wonder if we realize that idolatry extends beyond golden calves or the worship of false gods we hear so much about today. I even step on my own feet, because as I write this, I think of all of the things that I do that have nothing to do with God. I sit in front of my computer far too often playing games and listening to music. The music is 99% gospel, but even as I write this I realize that in many ways my computer has become an idol, as it takes up too much of my time. I'm not on the computer when I should be in church, but a lot of the time I spend on it could be spent praying, reading, teaching my children the Word, or anything of real significance. We all have something that takes up too much of our resources, be it our time, talents, or money. Search yourselves. Is there something in your own life that has the potential to be an idol? Perhaps you idolize an entertainer or sports figure? We must be careful to keep God #1 in our lives. With all of the distractions we have in this world, it has become increasingly difficult. Why does God have to be first? I'll try to keep that answer short. He is the Creator of Heaven and Earth. Before we were formed in the womb He knew everything about us and already had a plan for our lives. He has withheld no good thing from us, not even His Son. We owe Him nothing less, and in fact much more than we could ever give. Who else could provide us with eternal life? Who else can forgive sins? Who else could redeem us?

He wants to be #1 because He is worthy of being #1! Aside from that, putting Him first is best for us also. He has a good plan for our lives. He only wants what's best for us. If you believe this, put Him first, and obey Him in all things. I am personally resolving right now to waste less time on my computer, and spend more time taking care of kingdom business. What about you?

Selfish Ambition-Selfish ambition is when one seeks to achieve a goal at any expense (author's definition). We all have ambition. There is something that we all want to achieve while in this life. There is nothing wrong with ambition in and of itself. There is nothing wrong with wanting a good job and a good life. Here are three questions that can help you figure out if your ambition is normal or selfish: Why do I want this? Why am I doing this? What am I willing to do to achieve this goal? Be careful if the answer to your last question is anything. Those with selfish ambition care only for themselves and are willing to step on anyone to get what they want. They are willing to lie, cheat, steal, slander someone else's name, etc anything to get ahead. This is not God's will. God is an "others-centered" God. He cares so much about us that He didn't hold anything back....not even His only Son. He has a plan for our success, and that plan does not include hurting others in any way. We are meant to help each other. In this day and age, however, we talk about certain businesses being "cut throat" and how one has to "claw and scratch" their way to the top. Whose throat is being cut? Who receives the clawing and the scratching? Why does one have to succeed at another's expense? Is God not able to bless us all? Can we not go higher together?

Pride-This is when we think too highly of ourselves, it is to be arrogant or conceited (author's definition) "It's all about me;" "Look at what I can do;" "See how smart I am." "Why do I need God? I have my own plan for my life. It's all under control." A prideful person is his/her own god. Those who are filled with pride rely on themselves and their own wisdom (which, let's face it, is limited) and whatever gifts they possess to achieve their goals. A good example would be to look at some sports figures. Some are lifted up in pride in their own abilities. Never mind that their talent is given by God for His glory. Some of them use it for their own. One can tell those who are lifted up in pride by the outcome of their career. Are they better at the end than they were at the beginning? The Bible talks of how pride goes before a fall. How many can we say have fallen? They fall because they rely on themselves and not God. Those of us who are active in our churches should be careful to seek God's glory in all we do, and not our own. Think about why you sing in the choir, teach class, or whatever you do. Is God getting the glory or are you just trying to make a name for yourself? God does not look at just the works, he also looks at the motives. He looks at our hearts. In my own journey, on several occasions I have had to stop whatever I was doing and pray that God's will be done, that lives would be changed and that He would get the glory in whatever I do. It is also important to thank Him for every success that we experience in this life. I walked in pride throughout high school and college. I was so smart, I knew everything, and I had a good plan for my life (this is how I thought). In reality, it was pride that led me to make the worst mistakes of my life. Even now it is something that I have to guard myself against. If you are seeking your own glory, you are not seeking God's, and whatever you set out to do will ultimately fail. In Isaiah 42:8, the Lord says that He will not share his glory with another. This includes us. Keep your motives and your heart pure. God resists the proud but gives grace to the humble (Proverbs 3:34 or James 4:6 NIV). Let's rely on him and on his strength, which is limitless, instead of our own, which is limited. People who exalt themselves or anything else above God will not inherit His kingdom.

3) Witchcraft-You do this? Really?
And you call yourself a Christian?

As a born again child of God, I find it difficult to believe that anyone in the body of Christ would be involved in witchcraft. Apparently this is (and was) so, because it is mentioned more than once in the scriptures. Witchcraft manifests itself in many ways today: palm readers, false religions, tarot cards, and really even horoscopes. While God is all-powerful, and there is none greater than He, there are other powers at work. Anytime a person seeks to tap into these "other powers" that person is engaging in witchcraft. Spells and curses are real and are demonic in nature. Remember the "wise men" and sorcerers in Pharoah's court during Moses' time (Exodus 7:10-12)? Recall that King Saul consulted a spiritist to raise Samuel's spirit after the Lord rejected him as king in Israel (1st Samuel 28:7-25). Whose powers do you think these people were accessing? Certainly not the Lord's, when everything they were doing was in direct contrast to His will. That is witchcraft at its very core: rebellion. See for yourself by checking 1st Samuel 15:23. This is why Satan was cast out of heaven: pride and rebellion. For anyone practicing witchcraft of any sort, I warn you of the grave danger you are in if you do not repent. For those who consult people who do these things, you are in danger also, and not just eternally. Why follow vague horoscopes or listen to those who are in contact with spirits for guidance? God has all the answers that you will ever need. You won't need to consult a spiritual advisor. When He created you, He did it with a purpose. Why go to pretenders? He may use others to tell you things, but He also communicates directly with you. Let's not even go into casting spells and/or curses on people. God does not manipulate or dominate us and it is not His will for us to try and manipulate or dominate others. His will is that we all have free will. The very idea of trying to curse someone or even wishing evil upon them is a direct contrast to God's nature. He is love. We should reflect His love in our lives, even to our enemies. I warn you again, anyone involved in witchcraft in any way will find themselves left out of God's kingdom.

4) Hatred-You live this way? Really? And you call yourself a Christian?

"If anyone says 'I love God,' yet hates his brother, he is a liar. For anyone who does not love his brother, whom he has seen, cannot love God, whom he has not seen," 1st John 4:20 NIV. What more can I say? As previously stated, our God is a God of love. Hate is the exact opposite. It has no place in our lives. Some may say that this is easy for me to say, and I would agree. I have never been in a position to really hate anyone. I pray I never am in that sort of a position. However, I have heard extraordinary stories about people forgiving those who have killed or abused their children, so I know it is possible. It is impossible to forgive someone if you hate them. Hatred generally is the result of unresolved conflict. If someone does wrong, we are supposed to go to that person and show them their fault. How simple this is! How many hurt feelings or feelings of resentment could be avoided just by following this simple instruction? You see, God knows what's best for us. Why sit at home nursing a grudge when you could just tell the person of their fault? The sooner we handle conflict of any sort, the better off we are. In a practical sense, our bodies were not meant to carry around hatred. Think of someone you dislike (or possibly

even hate, though you shouldn't). How do you feel when you hear this person's name, or see them while out and about? Your breathing may become labored, you may feel "tight" in the chest, your blood pressure rises, and you probably tense up. Think of all the energy we use up on hate. I really believe some of the health problems people experience could have something to do with feelings of anger and/or hatred that just stay pent up in the body. We were not designed to carry all of that. It is not physically or spiritually healthy. God tells us what to do so that we won't have to carry it. Hatred can consume you if you let it. Guard your heart. If there is someone you think you hate, do good to them. Go out of your way if you have to. Pray for them. This is not for their sake, but for yours. This is not God's will for our lives. To be out of His will in this area will result in your being left out of His kingdom.

5) Discord, Dissensions, and Factions-You're a part of this? Really? And you call yourself a Christian?

"..Any kingdom divided against itself will be ruined, and a house divided against itself will fall," Luke 11:17 NIV. This was Jesus' response when he was accused of casting out demons by the power of Beelzebub (aka Satan). However, there is another important truth here: the power of unity which is the exact opposite of discord, dissensions, and factions.

Remember the story of the Tower of Babel (Gen. 11:1-8)? Take a look especially at verse 6, and see what the Lord says. They had one language and were united in purpose. The Lord confused their language because He knows that when a people are united in purpose, they are unstoppable. Nothing is impossible. These people were not doing God's will or seeking God's glory. God decided to stop them by creating different languages. Someone else knows about the power of unity: Satan. He knows that if he can keep God's people fighting and arguing among themselves, the work God intends for them to do will be greatly hindered, if not left completely undone.

Discord has three definitions, but only one that is relevant here (the others have to do with sound): lack of agreement, dissension.* Dissension is defined as a difference of opinion, especially one causing strife, within a group.* One of the definitions for faction is a cohesive, contentious minority within a larger group or internal dissension or discord.* See how all of the definitions are similar. These things can be prevalent in today's churches, if we as people of God are not careful. We must guard our own hearts and immediately address negative expressions when our brothers or sisters speak out against each other. The body of Christ can not function if it is fractured. A united church is a powerful church! This principle is true in every area of our lives, in our families, at work, in any organization. God meant for us to be united, to live in harmony with each other. What's wrong with this? Take a good, honest look at yourself. Do you know of any conflict or strife in any area of your life? Are you the cause? What about your church? Certainly you should make sure you are not the cause of any conflict or strife within the body of Christ. Those who start quarrels and keep mess going on in the church (and any other area of their lives as well) will find themselves left outside of God's kingdom.

6) Jealousy and Envy-This is in you? Really? And you call yourself a Christian?

"But if you harbor bitter envy and selfish ambition in your hearts, do not boast about it or deny the truth. Such "wisdom" does not come down from heaven, but is earthly, unspiritual, of

the devil. For where you have envy and selfish ambition, then you find disorder and every evil practice." James 3:14-16 NIV

Envy is defined as discontent and resentment aroused by desire for the possessions or qualities of another.* Why is this a sin? I'm not a scholar, but I can guess that first of all if one is focused on what someone else has, they are not focused on what they have. This is a way of telling God that what He has blessed them with is not good enough. Second, how do we treat people of whom we are inwardly jealous (be honest)? We are either "fake" with them or hostile, right? Is God not able to bless all of us abundantly? I found myself having to fight off jealousy when my sister bought her second home before I had even bought my first. She didn't buy a house that I wanted, it was just the fact that she bought and owned a home while I still rent my home. It was truly a fight, but when you resolve to live as God intends, He'll help you. It has been in my heart for years to buy a home, but circumstances made us wait. I knew it was wrong to be jealous, so I fought it, with the Lord's help. I knew that God can bless me in this manner the same way He blessed her (still waiting, but not much longer!). Does God not value everyone He made? So what if you can't preach, sing, or pray like someone else. So what if someone has that house or car or just seems to have their lives together while we struggle. We don't know what other people have been through to obtain what they have, or what they went through to become who they are. God made you for His good pleasure, to do His work. Stop looking at everyone else! What has God done for you? What do you believe He will do for you? Focus on what you have and who God made you to be. Think about it. How much fun is it to live in discontentment and resentment? Why waste time thinking about someone else and their possessions and/or qualities? Proverbs 14:30 (NIV) says that envy rots the bones. God doesn't want you to live this way. If you are jealous of someone for any reason, let it go now. As the song says, what God has for you is for you. God made you exactly how he wanted you to be. You are not superior or inferior to anyone else. Be who He made you to be, walk in His plan and provision for your life. There is no one else on earth exactly like you. So stop being jealous. There is no reason to envy anyone for any reason. Drop the jealousy and embrace your brother or sister. Be happy for them when they receive good things. Rejoice with them as if it were happening to you. Compliment them on the qualities they have that you like. Focus on yourself and how God loves you. Be content and be blessed. If you don't, you may find yourself left out of God's kingdom.

7) Fits of Rage-You do this? Really? And you call yourself a Christian?

"In your anger do not sin. Do not let the sun go down when you are angry, and do not give the devil a foothold." Eph. 5:26-27 NIV. We all get angry at some point in this life. Even Jesus got angry. It's what we do when we get angry that matters, which is why Paul said, "In your anger do not sin." People who don't heed these words generally are the ones who are quick to "blow their tops," or "go off on somebody." He also said not to let the sun go down while you are angry at someone. Why? Anger unabated turns to rage, and rage needs an outlet. Usually that means physical violence, though it could also manifest itself in verbal abuse. However one lets go of his or her rage, someone is apt to get hurt. It is not God's will for us to hurt each other. Read 1Cor 13. Does it say that love always hurts? Does it say that love leads to fits of rage? If someone makes you mad, must you really curse them out? Does there have to be a fight? Do we have to riot to express our anger? These reactions exhibit

blatant disobedience to God and his will for how we are supposed to live. Take a look at James 1:20 NIV, *"for man's anger does not bring about the righteous life that God desires."* Disobedience leaves us open to the oppression and influence of devils, which explains the last part of the scripture. We are supposed to be beacons of light for a dark and dying world. It is difficult for one who is in darkness to follow another in darkness. People in the dark follow whoever has the light. If you as a child of God act as a child of the devil, how can you influence anyone to follow Christ? Is there darkness in Him then? What if our Creator had fits of rage? Who could escape His wrath? I am thankful that God is not that kind of God and that he sets such a good example for us to follow. You can not act this way and honestly call yourself a child of God. If you are one of those people with a short fuse, repent now, or you will not inherit the kingdom of God.

8) Drunkenness-You do this? Really? And you call yourself a Christian?

"Wine is a mocker and beer a brawler; whoever is led astray by them is not wise," Prov. 20:1 NIV. There are numerous scriptures on drunkenness, but this one lays it out there. No matter what version of bible you have, this could not be clearer. Let's check out Prov. 23:29-35 NIV: *"Who has woe? Who has sorrow? Who has strife? Who has complaints? Who has needless bruises? Who has bloodshot eyes? Those who linger over wine, who go to sample bowls of mixed wine. Do not gaze at wine when it is red, when it sparkles in the cup, when it goes down smoothly! In the end it bites like a snake and poisons like a viper. Your eyes will see strange sights and your mind imagine confusing things. You will be like one sleeping on the high seas, lying on top of the rigging. 'They hit me,' you will say, 'but I'm not hurt! They beat me, but I don't feel it! When will I wake up so I can find another drink?"* The effects of drinking too

much are listed right in the scriptures. I have another one for you, look at Isaiah 5:22 NIV: *"Woe to those who are heroes at drinking wine and champions at mixing drinks."* So this is not just for those who drink but for those who mix the drinks. There is truly nothing new under the sun. The consequences of being hung over are listed above in Proverbs 23:29-35. Becoming drunk can result in arguing, fighting, and at the least, bloodshot eyes. Anyone who has ever been drunk can testify to this. Let's keep reading though. In verse 32 it says that "it bites like a snake and poisons like a viper." I take this to mean that it makes you sick (hence the vomiting, headaches, etc). Next verse, "your eyes will see strange sights and your mind imagine confusing (the KJV says perverse) things." Perhaps this is why people look differently when you wake up in the morning (you know what I mean!). Perhaps this is why some don't recall things that happen while they are intoxicated. Instead of reality, they see confusing (or perverse) things and strange sights. Moving on to verse 34, "you will be like one sleeping on the high seas, lying on top of the rigging (mast?)." I believe this refers to loss of balance, stumbling around, or something to that effect. Last verse: "they hit me, you will say, but I'm not hurt! They beat me but I don't feel it! When will I wake up so I can find another drink?" I believe we all know that alcohol is an anesthetic. There are a lot of things that have value that are misused. Most of what has been discussed here could also apply to drug use. Actually, alcohol is a drug.

So what makes drunkenness a sin? Read Eph. 5:18 NIV: "Do not get drunk on wine, which leads to debauchery...." Have you ever seen an intoxicated person do anything that glorifies God? Most people who are drunk are not in control of themselves. Have you ever heard of alcoholic beverages that are referred to as "spirits?" If you are not in control of yourself, who is? If you are under someone else's influence, how can you control yourself? Do you not know that Christ came to set free the captives? Why be in bondage to alcohol or drugs? Will God allow anyone to come staggering and intoxicated into His kingdom? Put the bottle down, and throw the drugs away before it is too late.

9) Lagniappe (a little extra)

"Furthermore, since they did not think it worthwhile to retain the knowledge of God, he gave them over to a depraved mind, to do what ought not to be done. They have become filled with every kind of wickedness, evil, greed, and depravity. They are full of envy, murder, strife, deceit and malice. They are gossips, slanderers, God-haters, insolent, arrogant and boastful; they invent ways of doing evil; they disobey their parents; they are senseless, faithless, heartless, ruthless. Although they know God's righteous decree that those who do such things deserve death, they not only continue to do these very things but also approve of those who practice them," Romans 1:28-32 NIV.

I would like to address four additional sins that have not been previously discussed: malice, deceit, greed and gossip. **Malice** is defined as a desire to harm others or to see others suffer.* Notice how most of the sins previously mentioned have the same theme at the core: lack of love for others. No matter what, no Christian has any business with malice in their hearts. If someone hurts you, the correct response is to forgive it and let it go. As a Christian, it will never be okay with God if we cheer for someone else's downfall. Instead we should be cheering for repentance and redemption. If you have malice in your heart, you do not have love. Love is of God, so where do you think malice comes from? **Gossip** -most of the scriptures that speak against gossip are in Proverbs. It is related to slander, as both have to do with saying things about other people that are likely false and usually malicious. Rarely do we say good things about people. Who has time to talk about someone's salvation, a graduation, or a promotion? These days most people would rather talk about who got who pregnant or who so-and-so is cheating on his/her spouse with. None of these things is encouraging or inspirational. There is no benefit to it. I would advise anyone who is a Christian or who wants to be one to read and heed Philippians 4:8. This is a good guide in thinking and in speaking, especially if one must speak about someone else. **Deceit** is the act of deceiving; to deliberately cause someone else to believe something that is not true (author's definition). This is one of the things that God hates (Prov. 6:16-19). People who lie can not be trusted, they have no credibility. Our God is a faithful God. Something that makes Him so amazing is that when He speaks a word to you, no matter what you do, He will not fail to do what He says He will do. People who practice deceit can not be relied upon for anything. The first part of Proverbs 26:28NIV says that a lying tongue hates those it hurts. Anyone in the habit of telling lies is basically practicing hatred. You literally hate the one you are lying to. We lie to ourselves when we say that a "little white lie" is harmless. As a Christian, one really has to be careful. If a Christian is caught in a lie (or in several lies), it damages their own reputation and that of God's, who they represent. We are His ambassadors. We represent Him on this earth, so we have to be above reproach in every area of our lives. People make enough excuses for not developing a relationship with Christ without us giving them another one. **Greed** (Luke 12:15-21, Prov. 15:27) is defined as an excessive desire for more than one needs or deserves.* Read the scriptures in Luke referenced above. See what's missing? This man had been blessed with more than he had room to receive. Apparently it did not even occur to him to share with others. In fact, in the law, God says to only go over your field once, and to leave whatever is left for those less fortunate (widows or children without fathers). This man decided to keep it all for himself. However, our Heavenly father, who made and owns everything, gives us freely anything we need. He does not withhold anything. So should it be with us. Why hold on to things when others are in need? Jesus said that a man's life does not consist in the abundance of his possessions. Those things people pursue (money and material possessions) will still be here when they leave this earth. We are just stewards or caretakers. So why is being greedy a sin? It violates both of Jesus's commands. He said that wherever your treasure is, there will your heart be. If you love money and material things, there is no love for God or for others (Matthew 6:21-24). Is it love to have food or clothes and not provide to someone who is in need (1st John 3:17-18)? Perhaps some of us need to see what it is like to be in need to understand this. Thank God that He isn't greedy! We'd all be in pitiful shape!

It would not be possible to go over every sin that there is in this book. I would be accused of killing a lot of trees! However the above scripture (Rom. 1:28-32 NIV) helps. The last part of the scripture definitely resonates with me, especially in today's time. It seems that we celebrate all the "wisdom" or "attributes" that are set up against the wisdom of God. Some examples: It's okay to retaliate when someone hurts you; if someone curses you, curse them back. It's okay to lie and cheat, take from others when you have a need. If someone upsets you, gossip behind their backs, slander their name. Why not sell drugs or sell other peoples' possessions so that you can buy the things that you want? Every man for himself! There are parades for those who choose an "alternative lifestyle." These lifestyles are becoming more and more acceptable, and certainly more popular than God's "old-fashioned" way. Jesus said that in the last days the love of many would wax cold. We are seeing that now, even here in the South, where we are supposed to be famous for our hospitality. It appears that society now celebrates what was once held as wrong (or sin) by everyone.

Sin begins in the heart. See Mark 7:21-22 NIV: *"For from within, out of men's hearts, come evil thoughts, sexual immorality, theft, murder, adultery, greed, malice, deceit, lewdness, envy, slander, arrogance and folly."* These were the words of Jesus. It begins in the heart, and a God-fearing person will kill it there and not let it manifest in our words or acts. You don't have to do everything that you think of. Most of us don't. It's more than not acting on our impulses, though. We have to repent of the thought itself. This is how you keep yourself pure. Cast the thought down and replace it with God's word. *"Submit yourselves, then, to God. Resist the devil, and he will flee from you,"* James 4:7 NIV. There would be much less sin if we did these things (submit and resist). Instead of resisting (assuming one is submitted to God in the first place) the enemy, we give in! Who's in control, the Spirit or the flesh? Search yourselves. The whole intent of this chapter is to allow you to check yourself to be sure that you are truly submitted to God in every area of your life, so that you may live eternally, and not be left "outside."

Chapter Three: Spotlight--
The Fruit of the Spirit

Galatians 5:22-23

We are meant to live like Jesus. He came to show us the way. Therefore, our example for this chapter and for the fruit of the spirit will be Jesus. All of the fruit mentioned in these scriptures was manifested in Him.

1) Love-You have this? That's good, because all Christians should!

".....But the greatest of these is love," 1st Corinthians 13:13b NIV. *"A new command I give you: Love one another. As I have loved you, so you must love one another. By this all men will know that you are my disciples, if you love one another,"* John 13:34-35 NIV. Jesus commanded us to love-God first and then each other (Matthew 22:37-39). One of the things I love most about our Savior is that he didn't command us to do something he didn't do himself. He loved his father, and he loved everyone he came in contact with. He showed his

love for his Father by obeying His will (see John 15:9-10). While he walked the earth, he showed his love for others by fellowship, healing, and delivering those who were demon-possessed. Did I forget to mention that he also died for all of us? He put us and our needs ahead of his own desires.

Most of us probably won't be put in a position where we are called upon to die in another's place. However, there are other ways to show love. We can give, volunteer our time and our talents, feed and clothe those less fortunate, and the list goes on. We can tell others about Jesus' love for us. Even better, we can show it. Loving others means to put them ahead of you and your priorities. Let's not get so wrapped up in ourselves that we have no time to help others. See 1st John 3:16-18 NIV, *"This is how we know what love is: Jesus Christ laid down his life for us. And we ought to lay down our lives for our brothers. If anyone has material possessions and sees his brother in need but has no pity on him, how can the love of God be in him? Dear children, let us not love with words or tongue but with actions and in truth."* So as you see, John was not talking about literally dying for others. He was really talking about sacrificing our own desires and priorities and helping someone else. Showing love involves more than an occasional hug or kiss. More action than that is needed.

We don't get to choose who we are to love, either. Jesus was not specific in who he said we have to love. We are to love everyone, no matter how we feel about them. If someone has wronged you, make the choice to forgive and move on. Don't allow anger or hatred to keep you out of heaven. Don't wait for a feeling that may never come. Forgive first and let the feeling (if you must have one) come later. See 1 John 3:14-15, *"We know that we have passed from death to life, because we love our brothers. Anyone who does not love remains in death. Anyone who hates his brother is a murderer, and you know that no murderer has eternal life in him."* How are you doing in the love department?

2) Joy-You have this? That's good, because all Christians should!

"I have told you this so that my joy may be in you and that your joy may be complete," John 15:11 NIV. *"Rejoice in the Lord always. I will say it again: Rejoice!"* Philippians 4:4. Jesus walked in joy. Before he was crucified, he instructed his disciples to remain in his love that his joy would be in them and that it may be complete. Jesus had joy because he remained in his father's love. In the presence of the Lord, there is "fullness of joy." Jesus was always in the presence of his Father, and he always had joy. See Luke 10:17-21. After Jesus heard the report of his disciples, he was filled with joy through the Holy Spirit. It was joy that enabled Jesus to go to the cross (Hebrews 12:2 NIV). He endured the cross because he saw joy on the other side as he knew he would return to heaven and would be seated at the right hand of God. We are meant to have joy regardless of our circumstances. I've lived long enough to know that sometimes that is easier said than done. See John 15:33b:"In this world you will have trouble. But be of good cheer (or rejoice!), I have overcome the world." Those of us who are in Christ really have a reason to rejoice. Nothing we face is greater than He. Whatever the situation, remember that the joy of the Lord is your strength (Nehemiah 8:10). Cast your care on him and rejoice in the victory he has won for you! Why would anyone want to be a Christian when most of the Christians they know walk around with long faces? Some look as if they have made a career of sucking on lemons! We have a future and a hope (Jer. 29:11)! We are more than conquerors through Christ Jesus (Romans 8:37)! Let the joy of the Lord shine through

you. Let those who don't know Jesus (especially those who know you and whatever challenges you are facing) see your joy in spite of what you are going through. Proclaim victory and rejoice even in your darkest hour. This is what sets you apart. This is what makes you peculiar. Rejoice!

3) Peace-You have this?
That's good, because all Christians should!

"Peace I leave with you, my peace I give you. I do not give to you as the world gives. Do not let your hearts be troubled and do not be afraid," John 14:27 NIV. *"And the peace of God, which transcends all understanding, will guard your hearts and your minds in Christ Jesus."* Philippians 4:7 NIV. While Jesus walked the earth, He was at peace. The only time we see Jesus troubled and sorrowful was when he knew the time of his suffering and crucifixion was at hand. Even then, after praying and settling things within himself, He came back to that place of peace. By the time the crowd got to Him, he was no longer troubled. He set out to fulfill all that had been written about Him in scripture. He gave us his peace. We are not meant to live in fear or anxiety.

Peace is defined in several ways: the absence of war or other hostilities (how we are supposed to live with each other); an agreement or treaty to end hostilities; freedom from quarrels and disagreement; harmony; public security and order, and last (and my favorite), serenity (or peace of mind).* See Philippians 4:6-7 NIV: *"Do not be anxious about anything, but in everything, by prayer and petition, with thanksgiving, present your requests to God. And the peace of God, which transcends all understanding, will guard your hearts and your minds in Christ Jesus."* Whatever we have need of, pray and ask God. If you prayed according to God's will and believe that He will answer your prayer (meaning you prayed in faith), He will give you His peace. It won't even matter how He answers the prayer. It is a blessed thing to trust in the Lord. People who trust God for everything sleep well at night. People who trust God don't have to knock on doors, call on family members or friends, take out payday loans, go to casinos or buy lottery tickets. There's no need for drugs or alcohol to block out pain or anxiety. All we have to do is let God work and be ready to do our part. Are you worrying or anxious because of something or someone? Give it to God. His peace is available to you today.

4) Patience-You have this? That's good, because all Christians should!

"But for that very reason I (Paul-added by author) was shown mercy so that in me, the worst of sinners, Christ Jesus might display his unlimited patience as an example for those who would believe on him and receive eternal life," 1st Timothy 1:16 NIV. The same patience Jesus had for Paul, he has for each of us. If he can have patience with us, he who gave his all for us, should we not be patient with each other? As a mother, I have often told my children that my patience was wearing thin. When they heard that, they knew that it was time to straighten up. Thank God that Jesus is not like me! No matter how much we fall or fail, He is patient with us. We may have to experience his discipline from time to time, but he has never treated us as our actions (or inactions) deserve. So, as a Christian, we should not "fly off the handle" whenever things don't go our way. If something happens to upset us, take a deep breath and handle it! Remember that we all have faults. We should bear with one another in love.

We should also learn to have patience while waiting for manifestations of promises God has spoken to us. Remember Abraham's wife Sarah? She was told she would bear a son. As I understand it, it was approximately 25 years from when they received the promise and when the promise was manifested. During that time, Sarah apparently got tired of waiting and decided to help God out. The result was a mess that continues to this day. There are several scriptures that tell us to wait, be patient, be long suffering, and endure. If we would do just that, we would receive everything God has in store for us at just the right time. When we become impatient and take matters into our own hands, that is when we tend to mess things up. Let God do his work his way. Remember that His way is the best way. Just be patient.

5) Kindness-You have this? That's good, because all Christians should!

"I will tell of the kindnesses of the Lord, the deeds for which he is to be praised, according to all the Lord has done for us-yes, the many good things he has done for the house of Israel, according to his compassion and many kindnesses," Isaiah 63:7 NIV. *"but let him who boasts boast about this: that he understands and knows me, that I am the Lord, who exercises kindness, justice and righteousness on earth, for in these I delight, declares the Lord,"* Jeremiah 9:24 NIV. While Jesus walked the earth, He showed kindness in so many different ways. Remember the leper he touched (Luke 5)? How about the man at the synagogue with the withered hand (Luke 6)? Surely you remember the woman with the issue of blood (Mark 5:21-34)? I could go on and on citing all of the recorded acts that showed kindness manifested in Jesus' ministry here on earth. See Matthew 9:36 NIV: *"When he (Jesus-added by author) saw the crowds, he had compassion on them, because they were harassed and helpless, like sheep without a shepherd."*

Kind is defined as of a generous or warm-hearted nature; showing sympathy and understanding; humane.* How about us? How do we show kindness? There are at least two ways: in speech and in deed. See the following scripture references: Proverbs 12:25; Proverbs 19:17, Daniel 4:27, 1st Thessalonians 5:15, and Ephesians 4:32. Who do we show kindness to? In a word: everyone. We don't choose who to be kind to anymore than we choose who to love. It's easy to be kind to those who are kind to us, those who love us, and possibly even the needy. We are ordered to be kind to everyone, just like our Heavenly Father (Luke 6:35).

6) Goodness-You have this? That's good, because all Christians should!

"Taste and see that the Lord is good..." Psalm 34:8. *"I am the good shepherd...."* John 10:11. Goodness is the state and quality of being good.* There are many definitions of good: being positive or desirable in nature; having desirable qualities; suitable, appropriate; virtuous; upright; benevolent; kind, etc (not all definitions listed).* Jesus is all this and more. While he walked the earth, his goodness showed in his interaction with others and in his works (Acts 10:38).

How do we know if we are good? Jesus said that only God is good (Matthew 19:17, Mark 10:18, Luke 18:19). So in and of ourselves, there is nothing good in us. Since goodness is a fruit of the Spirit, our goodness comes from the Holy Spirit within us. The Holy Spirit came from Jesus, who is the Son of God. Therefore we have His goodness in us.

So how do we determine a person's goodness? Is it by our works? We have to be careful when we look at the actions of others. There are some who do good things to be "seen of men," but are not necessarily good people. Consider someone like a drug dealer or a bank robber. Most of them do many good things, like giving money to those less fortunate. They can be caring and loving, especially towards their own families. However, they make a living robbing and poisoning others (let's just call it what it is) and destroying lives. Where's the goodness in that? I think someone who does something like that does the good works to appease their conscious. We only see the good deeds, but God sees the heart. He sees the motives behind the work. We have to make sure that whatever we do, we are doing it out of our love for God. Our good deeds should come from the goodness of our hearts. They are not intended to be our goodness. The goodness should already be there. One should not say "I am good because I give money and donate clothes to the poor," but rather "I give money and donate clothes to the poor because I am good." A good person is genuinely caring and concerned about others, how God meant for us to be. The works should be evidence of the goodness that is already there (see Luke 6:45). If a person is rotten inside but does good things, eventually the true nature will come to light (see Proverbs 26:24-26). Love God first, then each other (including our enemies). If you do this, the goodness will follow.

7) Faithfulness-You have this? That's good, because all Christians should!

".....for the faithfulness of the Lord endures forever...." Psalm 117:2 NIV. *"Therefore holy brothers, who share in the heavenly calling, fix your thoughts on Jesus, the apostle and high priest whom we confess. He was faithful to the one who appointed him, just as Moses was faithful in all God's house,"* Hebrews 3:1-2 NIV. To be faithful is to be reliable, trustworthy, and believable (author's definition). While Jesus walked the earth, was he ever proven to be unfaithful? Take a look at some of his acts of healing. He told the centurion and the father of a child to go and that the people they sought healing for had received it. What would have happened to his ministry if these people got home and found their loved ones in worse condition than before or even dead? We always talk about how fast bad news gets around. Take a

look at the ten lepers. Jesus did not heal them immediately. He told them to go and show themselves to the priest. They took Him at his word and left. They were healed as they went. What do you think would have happened if they got to the priest and still had leprosy? In this day and age, they would have been calling newspapers, blogging on the internet, and shouting from the mountaintop that Jesus was a fraud. They believed his word, and Jesus was proven to be faithful to his word. He is still faithful to his word, even to this day. All we have to do is believe it.

Faithfulness is defined as adhering firmly and devotedly, loyal; worthy of trust, reliable; accurate and true.* See Hebrews 3:1-2 again. Jesus was appointed to come to earth and offer himself as a sacrifice for sin. Thank God that he was faithful to that task! Thank God that Jesus could be trusted with something so important. How about us? Are we faithful to the task(s) to which God appoints us? I personally would not want someone to say of me "You can't believe a word out of her mouth," or "She said she would be here, but you know how she is. She may be here and she may not be." Are we not faithful when it comes to working for a paycheck? What we do for God is so much more important. Perhaps we don't see it this way because we don't always see immediate rewards, but it is. We should be faithful in every area of our lives. Show God that He can trust you. Do your job. Be honest. Do what you say you will do, and don't commit to anything you know you can't do. Remember the parable of those who were given talents by their master (Matthew 25:14-30).

8) Gentleness-You have this? That's good, because all Christians should!

"Take my yoke upon you and learn from me, for I am gentle and humble in heart, and you will find rest for your souls,"

Matthew 11:29 NIV. *"Let your gentleness be evident to all..."* Philippians 4:5 NIV. Gentleness is defined as considerate or kindly; not harsh or severe; soft, mild; easily managed or handled, docile.* I don't know much about the other religions of this world and their requirements. However, I do know that Jesus only had two commandments: in short, to love God and love each other. We don't have any rituals, no required number of prayers or righteous acts to perform. There are no mandated periods of fasting and certainly no sacrifices to perform. All we have to do is love (and in some cases that is enough). To see how gentle Jesus was, look at how he treated "sinners." Recall the woman who was caught in the very act of adultery (John 8:4-11). He was the only one present who had a right to throw a stone at her, because he was the only one present that was without sin. Not only did he not throw a stone, he didn't even condemn her. He wasn't even harsh with her. He just told her to go and sin no more. On the Day of Judgment, when the disobedient are sent to their eternal destination, I believe that even then he will not be harsh with them. I imagine that he will most likely be grieving. We are meant to be the same way. Instead of being harsh with people, we should bear with each other in love (notice how love seems to be involved in all of the fruit?). None of us are perfect. Let's be as gentle to each other as we would want someone to be with us.

9) Self-Control-You have this? That's good, because as a Christian, you need it!

"So then, let us not be like others, who are asleep, but let us be alert and self-controlled," 1st Thessalonians 5:6 NIV. *"For the grace of God that brings salvation has appeared to all men. It teaches us to say* **NO** *to ungodliness and worldly passions, and to live self-controlled, upright and godly lives in this present age,"* Titus 2:11-12 NIV. I am no bible scholar, so if there is

a specific scripture that speaks to Jesus' self control, I have not found it. We know that Jesus lived a sinless life which any of us knows takes a degree of self-control that we do not possess. However, there are two instances in Jesus' life on earth where we see His self-control on display. The first was when he was tempted at the beginning of His ministry. The second was at the end of his ministry, when he was scourged and then crucified.

Take a look first at Matthew 4:1-11. There are some of us who could possibly resist the temptation to command stones to become bread after fasting 40 days on their own strength (I'm not one of them). I hope none of us would leap off of any high point with the belief that God would send an angel to catch us. Rebuke the devil if you hear a voice telling you to jump off of any high point. That is not God! The real test would be the last one. How many of us could honestly say that we would not accept all the kingdoms of the world if they were offered? If you think you would say no to the last question, let me ask you another: do you play the lottery? Do you go to casinos? Surely you don't spend your time and money at the casinos hoping to lose. You may not be able to obtain all the kingdoms of the world through gambling, but the motives behind it are the same: greed, pride, love of money and material possessions. Our example, Jesus, did not yield to temptation. At his physically weakest moment, he remained in control of himself. Let's fast-forward to the garden of Gethsemane (beginning at Matthew 26:38). Jesus did ask that the cup pass from Him, but He did not shy away from what He knew God wanted him to do, no matter how his flesh struggled. Honestly, I believe that Jesus was tempted that night also. He could have escaped the coming darkness (see Matthew 26:53). He could have turned away from this part of his assignment and called on the angels.

Thank God he didn't! He stayed in control of his flesh, but what a fight it must have been (see Luke 22:43-44).

We are called to be self-controlled also. Perhaps you have noticed that this "fruit" is in direct contrast to most of the sins identified in the previous chapter (i.e. sexual immorality, drunkenness, fits of rage, etc). If we remain in control of ourselves, we won't engage in these things. Too many of us, however, are the opposite. We are controlled instead of being in control. How many times have you heard someone talking about needing something (i.e. sex, alcohol, or drugs)? Is it really a need, or is it just a desire of the flesh? A need is something you can not live without, or at least something that it would be difficult to live without (i.e. water). A drink is not a need. Sex is not a need (especially if you are not married). You don't need that hit. Those "needs" do not have to be fulfilled. Conquer your flesh and make it submit to God and His will for your life. On its own, the flesh does not want to do God's will. For example, my church has corporate prayer on Saturday mornings. I did not go at first because I wanted my extra couple of hours of sleep. I told myself that I worked hard all week and that Saturday was my only day to sleep in. The problem is that I was so used to being up early that I would just be lying in bed, eyes wide open. My flesh just did not want to get up and go to church. It took awhile, but I have conquered my flesh and as long as I am in town, I am in church on Saturday mornings. I had to make up my mind that I was going, and even when the bed seemed so warm and inviting, I got up. If I can do it, you can to. That is a minor example, but if we are going to do God's will in every area of our lives, we must control the bodies we live in. God knows how hard this is for us, which is why he provided the Holy Spirit, who lives within. He is our guide, and trust me when I tell you He will let you know if you are going the wrong way or doing the wrong thing. We are not without help, so let's use it!

10) Lagniappe-Life with Jesus

A person can exhibit all of the Fruit of the Spirit and still not be saved without the most important thing: a relationship with Jesus Christ (Rev. 3:20, Matthew 7:22-23). It's not enough to imitate Him, we need to get to know Him (Matthew 11:29). This happens through regular church attendance, and setting aside time to pray and to read. We also have to obey His teachings and commands. Read His word and learn how to live this life His way. This is a daily thing, not one day a week, or once every few months. Obedience to God's word is key. Submission to His will is key. It is how you do in this area that will determine if you are a "sheep" or a "goat" (Matthew 25:32). Love the Lord your God and acknowledge Jesus as your personal Lord and Savior. Once you do this and it has become real to you, the submission and obedience will follow. If you found your shortcoming(s) in the previous chapter (I found more than one), resolve now to STOP doing whatever it is and ask the Lord to help you to live according to His will. Believe me, He will. You can then know that you are a Christian, and you can rest in the knowledge of your eternal destination.

Chapter Four: Choices and Consequences

Joshua 24:15, Deuteronomy 30:19-20

Here is the whole chapter in one phrase: obey-live; disobey-die. That's what sin is, disobedience to God's word. Hopefully by now you can see a difference between living a sinful life and living a sinless life. You have a choice to make and there is no fence. You can not please God and satisfy the desires of your flesh. One will have to go. You must choose. God did not create robots. It pleased Him to give us free will because He wants us to want Him. Deep down, we all want Him. We all have a deep yearning for something more than just the fulfillment of our dreams and the things of this life. Nothing else will ever fill the hole within us. The problem is we seek to fill it in other ways. God is the answer. He is what's missing in your life. With Him, there is no mid-life crisis. There is no need for drugs or alcohol. There is no need to seek love through a one night stand with a person you just met at the club.

In my eyes, the choice is easy. Who wants to die? The thought of being separated from the One who loves me more than anyone else ever could terrifies me, never mind the horror of an eternal Hell. In the presence of God is "fullness of joy," love, peace, and all of the fruit mentioned above. When you have those things working in your life, you live without worry or fear. Choose to obey Him and abide in His love. Live in the place of being whole, healed, and in abundance. Will there be trouble? Of course! Even then, as a true child of the King, you will have His help. You will not be forsaken, and there is no one greater than God. You may have to go through some things, but there is always victory on the other side.

So what is the alternative? What do you have to gain by continuing to live in a life of sin? In the long run: nothing. Death. There may be fun for awhile, but it always ends in death (Romans 6:23). Check those scriptures that were given at the beginning of Chapter 3: 1st Corinthians 6:9, Ephesians 5:3, Colossians 3:5, Rev. 21:8, and Rev. 22:15. All of those scriptures point to what happens to those who continue to sin and do wrong in God's sight. Really, it is shown throughout the bible: blessings for obedience, and curses or death to the disobedient. Keep drinking-death to the body (brain cells, liver, etc). Keep taking drugs-death to the body (brain cells, possible stroke, overdose, etc). Keep having sex outside of marriage-disease, unwanted pregnancies and the drama that comes with it-delay to a dream because resources now have to go towards paying medical bills or raising a child, and the list goes on. Keep stealing-death to your freedom and you will eventually lose everything you thought was worth having. Keep hating, keep being jealous, and keep living in pride - death. There will be death to relationships (a prideful person exalts him/herself above all others), death to dreams, and eventually physical death . Keep seeking the spirits for your answers-death. Those very spirits you consult will likely be the death of you. They don't care anything about you. They just want you dead outside of Christ. They're going down and their purpose is to take you with them. Live your life of sin without true repentance and its subsequent change-eternal death which is separation from God. Expect to live for all eternity without love, without peace, without joy. Expect to live in a place where no one cares for you, and no one cares what happens to you. Expect to live in a place of torment. Expect to burn. Expect no end to it.

Please don't deceive yourselves. When the letters in the New Testament were written, they were written to believers, not to those who had not yet come to Christ. There is life after death. We were all created in the image of God. He is spirit, and so are we. He is immortal and so are we. The flesh and blood will die, but it is just an outer covering, a shell. Our spirits will live on. How your spirit will live for all eternity is up to you. If you are one of those who think that God is too good to send people to hell, you are right. I saw a church sign that says it all: "God does not send people to hell, He just honors their choice." One of my pastors used to say, "If you die and go to hell, you ought to be happy about it." Obviously no one would be happy to go there, but this is what some of us will be choosing if we refuse to obey God's will and His word. This is the most important decision you will ever make. It is more important than where to go to college, what job to take, who to marry, when or whether you want to have children, etc. If you seek God's kingdom first, He will help you to make those other decisions. He can't help you, though, if you don't choose to follow Him. Your decision is eternal. Stop playing with eternity and get off the fence!

Conclusion: No Condemnation

Romans 8:1, 1st Corinthians 6:11

This book was never intended to judge or condemn anyone. It is only meant to show how even believers can be deceived into thinking that they are okay with God because they go to church, and maybe even serve in certain capacities within the church. It is more than that. We can't be hearers only. We must obey. If you feel a bit defensive after reading this, it is probably because you're feeling some conviction. Instead of fighting it, give in. Don't justify your sin. Repent of it. Confess your sin to God and seek His forgiveness. He'll give it (1st John 1:9). Jesus already came to die for us. See Hebrews 10:26. He won't come to die again. Jesus said it on the cross: "It is finished." His work is done. It is time for us to do our part. We believe, and that's where most of us stop. We also have to receive Him and become the person He meant us to be. You, as a believer, have been given the Spirit of God and the mind of Christ. Let go of the worldly lifestyle. Repent and yield yourself to the Lord. He will not turn you away.

We all make mistakes, but we don't have to wallow in them like pigs in mud. If we sin against God, just repent and try harder not to sin again. He knows us. He sees our condition. He knows that we can't help ourselves. That's why He sent Jesus. Since Jesus came and died for us, we now have access to His grace. While we live this life, we will not be completely sinless. On the other hand, we should not be pursuing a sinful lifestyle. The Bible is clear on what sin is, and God has not changed His mind. Sin can not abide in God's presence. Think of Isaiah's response when he saw the Lord sitting on His throne (Isaiah 6:1-5). Think of Peter's response during one of his first encounters with Jesus (Luke 5:8). They knew what we appear to have forgotten: to see the Lord in their natural sinful bodies usually meant death. We live in the era of God's grace, but it should not be taken for granted.

If we give over our will and yield to Him, we will sin less, and be quicker to repent. It will be easier to stay clean. This is your chance now. Be the Christian you claim to be. Lay aside those habits and lifestyles that you know are contrary to God's word. Let God's will prevail in your life. This is your chance to start over. Unfortunately, there is nothing we can do about what is already done. However, we still have today. Commit yourself right now to live according to God's word in every area of your life. If you're ready to do that, pray with me now: *Heavenly Father, I am so sorry for how I have represented you. Please forgive me for my sin(s) of _____. I ask you to create in me a clean heart and to renew a right spirit within me. I give my life to you. Make me the person you always meant for me to be. Teach me your word. I resolve right now to obey your word and to pattern my life after your word, no matter what. Lead me, guide me, and keep me from all wrong. Lord I thank you for forgiveness and for a fresh start. I am your child now, in spirit and in truth. Help*

me to represent you better and use me for your service. In Jesus'
name I pray, Amen.

If you sincerely prayed that prayer, I have only two more things to say: Welcome back Christian and get ready to fulfill God's plan for your life!

Works Cited

*Definitions obtained from <u>The American Heritage Dictionary</u>, 3rd Ed. 1994.

HOLY BIBLE, NEW INTERNATIONAL VERSION. Copyright 1973, 1978, 1984 by International Bible Society. Used by permission of Zondervan. All rights reserved.